I0751614

ladle. paleo and gluten-free comfort soups

disclaimer

The content presented in this book is meant for informational purposes only. The purchaser of this book understands that the author is not a medical professional, and the information contained within this book is not intended to replace medical advice or meant to be relied upon to treat, cure, or prevent any disease, illness, or medical condition. It is understood that you will seek full medical clearance by a licensed physician before making any changes mentioned in this book. The author claims no responsibility to any person or entity for any liability, loss, or damage caused or alleged to be caused directly or indirectly as a result of the use, application, or interpretation of the material in this book.

credits

Written and Photographed by Michelle Fagone, Cavegirl Cuisine, LLC
Editor: Leslie Auman, The Whole Life Balance
Cover Design and Layout: Vivian Cheng, Blend Creations

Printed in the United States of America

Sunny Day Publishing, LLC
Akron, Ohio 44333
www.sunnydaypublishing.com

ISBN 978-0-9903823-7-9
Library of Congress Control Number: 2016941168

paleo and gluten-free comfort soup recipes

by Michelle Fagone, aka "Cavegirl"
of CavegirlCuisine.com

To Laura Rivers: Cheers to hippie chicks, long phone conversations, wacky children, patient husbands, cheap wine, bumper stickers, old cookbooks...and a great friendship.

table of contents

introduction

introduction

Dear Cavepeeps,

I have been blogging about the Paleo and gluten-free lifestyle as Cavegirl Cuisine since March of 2012. The learning curve has been non-stop, not only in the blogosphere and figuring out the ins and outs but also in creating recipes that are attractive and tasty to my folks. Among the many hats a food blogger must wear (e.g. photographer, marketer, writer), the most important one is a recipe creator. I have learned so much about fresh and unusual ingredients, as well as many kitchen tricks. Through my posts and social media interaction, my audience and I have shared so much together.

If you are new to this lifestyle, there are in-depth science-type breakdowns for you all over the Internet. However, in a nutshell, the theory is that you are better off living life like your ancestors, the cave folks. Meat was hunted. Berries, nuts, fruits, and veggies were foraged. To bring it around to this century, basically, eliminate processed food and eat whole, fresh foods as often as possible. Grains are a no-no across the board. They just contain too many inflammatory properties. As a rule of thumb, Paleo folks generally do not eat legumes (lectins) and dairy, but check your gut health. If dairy does not bother you, then incorporating a little real, fresh, non-processed cheeses or heavy creams into some of your recipes is not a deal-breaker. This is *your* lifestyle. Figure out what works for you. Figure out what makes your body feel good.

Soups have hands-down become my favorite meal to make over the past several years. No matter your lifestyle or diet or restrictions, soup fits right in. I like to think of soup as a transitional meal. So many times, especially as women, we will decide to follow a "diet," and the only reception from our family is a bunch of groans. The great thing about the Paleo lifestyle is that it naturally includes meats and healthy produce. How can you go wrong with this combination? No more making a meal of a dry chicken breast and bland broccoli for yourself while your family chows down on some mac-n-cheese. Teach them to eat healthy. Fix only one meal. Introduce your family members to new foods while at the same time keeping some things familiar...like chicken, beef, celery, onions, tomatoes, and just a great, flavorful broth. That's not so scary, right?

Fresh veggies, clean meats, seafood, and fresh herbs and seasonings fill not only your bowls but also the house with smells of comfort and home. Over the pages of this book, I hope you will learn to create fabulous soup bases and incorporate your favorite additions to create some hearty and soulful bowls of love!

Happy Eating,

Michelle

Michelle Fagone, "Cavegirl"

why soup?

why soup?

The question should be, "Why *not* soup?" These bowls of warmth can be inexpensive, comforting, healthy, and quick meals. Soups can also be a great "transition" meal for someone wanting to adopt a Paleo and gluten-free lifestyle with a family that may not be so receptive to the idea. By utilizing fresh veggies, herbs, and meats, there is something for everyone.

soup for budgets

Although some soups can certainly be expensive, depending on the ingredients, traditionally, they have been a meal that can be cooked with leftovers from the week. Once you get the hang of it, you will start to understand what spice and vegetable combination make your taste buds happy. Instead of letting those last few bulbs of garlic rot or letting the produce in your crisper wilt and turn brown, chop them up, add some herbs and spices, throw in some broth, and there you go...a wonderful meal created from ingredients that may have been thrown away. Add ground beef or chicken thighs to your soup as a less expensive protein to round out a meal and hit all of the macronutrients the body needs...fats (from the cooking oil), proteins (from the meat), and carbohydrates (from the veggies).

soup for comfort

While spring and summer soups are refreshing to make after a trip to the farmer's market, during the fall and winter is when soups really warm the body...and the heart! Having a big pot of soup or chili cooking all day warms the house and allows family members to ladle a bowl whenever the need strikes. There is nothing better than a bowl of creamy soup by the fireplace after a snowball fight. But most importantly, a good bowl of soup can take us back to beautiful memories of our parents, grandparents, and family gatherings. Even though my mom never made soups from scratch, when I was sick she always warmed up a can of Cream of Mushroom or Cream of Tomato soup...you know the brand! Although it wasn't homemade, it is a beautiful memory, remembered with love.

soup for health

There have been many arguments whether chicken soup is good for a cold, but we definitely know that it is good for the soul. The steam opens up our sinuses, and it is warm and soothing. Even when we're not sick, soups are a healthy, proactive addition to any diet. Just like salads, it is one of the few ways we generally will eat such a variety of vegetables in one sitting. Fresh herbs and organic vegetables deliver a wealth of vitamins and minerals. Although you or your family may not enjoy consuming vegetables alone during a meal, the mix of flavors and spices in soups makes them more satisfying. In addition, because soups are nutrient-dense, they are filling, and the tendency to overeat decreases.

soup for the busy cook

Soups are great for rounded meals of nutrition in about 30 minutes. You can even reduce the prep time for weekday meals by prepping your veggies and making broth one day a week for your line-up of recipes. Most soups start with sautéing onions and other specific vegetables. After that, it is just adding the broth, meats, and seasonings. Next, you cover and simmer for 30 minutes while you take care of other business. Also, you can take advantage of your slow cooker with many soup recipes so that dinner can be ready when you walk in the door. And, honestly, this is my favorite way, because the flavors really have a chance to marry together and magnify by dinnertime...the taste is exponentially better the next day!

Cavegirl Tip: *If you are tired of half-used containers of fresh herbs going to waste, or if your garden is overflowing, make herb cubes to use throughout the year. Place about 2–3 teaspoons of chopped fresh herb leaves in each compartment of an ice cube tray. Personally, I like the silicone versions as the ice cubes are easier to pop out. Fill the tray with water just covering the herbs. Freeze until solid. Label individual freezer bags with the name of the herb and place cubes in appropriate bag. When making soups or stews throughout the year, drop a cube or two into your broth.*

kitchen soup essentials

kitchen soup essentials

Colander or Sieve

When making homemade broths, you will need a tool to help strain out the bones, herbs, and vegetables. I love a coarse-meshed sieve for this task; however, if you use a colander, just make sure your holes aren't so large that the bits get through. If your pasta pot hasn't seen much action since living the Paleo lifestyle, dust it off. It is great for the initial strain, as there is already a built-in colander that can remove the larger pieces, such as bones and chopped vegetables.

Cutting Boards

Without a cutting board, prep work pretty much can't be done. Because soups require preparing your vegetables, meats, and herbs, a quality cutting board (or two) is a kitchen essential. I keep a large wooden board on my kitchen counter for the everyday kitchen prep of vegetables, fruits, and herbs. I also own a couple of plastic cutting boards, both large and small, that I use for meat prep. Because of meat contamination, plastic cutting boards can be easily thrown in the dishwasher for a high-heat cleaning.

Dutch Oven

Since starting my Paleo journey, soups have become an essential meal in our family. With that, my Dutch oven has been extra loved. Dutch ovens are durable and heavy. This heaviness allows for an even cooking temperature, provides a great searing vessel, and is perfect for one-pot meals. Make the investment. It is absolutely worth it.

Immersion Blender

Paleo soups are generally void of heavy creams, so blended vegetables are used to obtain that creamy, silky texture. Although you can transfer batches of soup to a stand blender to achieve this same silkiness, an immersion blender used directly in the pot of hot soup is a nice luxury for a reasonably-priced kitchen tool. It not only helps cut down on mess but also immersion blenders are available in so many pretty colors!

Ladle

Now, come on. Did you think I would overlook this book's namesake? Ladles are the perfect vessel for transferring hot soups to individual soup bowls. Period. A large kitchen spoon can be used, but you usually have hot overflow spillage, and you sometimes miss of lot of the veggie and meat chunks that are crucial to the meal!

Sharp Knives

Dull knives are the most dangerous tool in the kitchen because they require more pressure when cutting through food. This can cause a loss of control and a possible accident. Good knives can be expensive; however, you do not have to run out and buy a full set of top-of-the-line knives. Find a brand that you like and purchase one at a time and slowly expand your collection. My suggestion would be to start with an 8-inch chef's knife as, personally, I find it to be the most versatile.

Slow Cooker

Slow cookers are a great kitchen appliance for the busy person or family. You can throw everything in it in the morning and come home at night to a warm, balanced meal. Slow cookers are also the perfect appliance for bone broth, as it takes at least 10 hours to cook.

Soup Storage

Well-lidded glass and BPA-free plastic containers are essential for storing your soups and broths in the refrigerator and freezer. Invest in different sizes. In addition to larger storage containers, having frozen one-serving portions is convenient and makes it easy to thaw out a nice meal overnight in the refrigerator for the next day.

fresh broths

fresh broths

I firmly believe and stand behind that the secret to a great soup, stew, or bisque is the broth, the very base of the recipe. It is the foundation to build on all of the other flavors. Broths can be easily made and are an inexpensive delicacy that you will oftentimes see steaming in a large stock pot in the kitchens of most fancy restaurants. Although soups and stews are the obvious use, broths can be excellent additions in sauces, a base liquid for steaming vegetables, adding to vegetable mashes instead of milk, and in braising liquids for meats.

I roast a chicken each Sunday (well, okay, *some* Sundays), which is my prep day. Then I peel the meat off of the carcass and refrigerate the chicken. Next, I make my broth from the chicken bones. I not only have chicken already prepared to be eaten straight out of the container or to be used in a recipe, but I also have fresh broth to make a soup that week. Between the recipe using the chicken, the soup, and some leftovers, our family of four can get 3–5 meals out of this. It is healthy, quick, and good! On a side note, you can transform the chicken a thousand different ways and pretty much come up with that many soup combinations as well. So, if your family likes variety, it can be accomplished easily.

My recipes are merely guidelines. If you do not have celery in the refrigerator, make the broth anyway. It will work just fine. Also, there is no need to discard those vegetable ends during the week. When chopping bell peppers, carrots, celery, and onions, there are always those odd ends that generally get thrown away. Keep a bag in your refrigerator. These odd bits can be used in preparing your broth at the end of the week.

Directions:

For the broths, simply place ingredients in a stock pot or Dutch oven. Add 6 cups of water (plus a few extra tablespoons to allow for steaming). Bring to boil. Reduce heat and simmer covered for 2–3 hours. Remove from heat and let cool. Strain liquid and discard the rest. This should yield six cups. Broth is good refrigerated for about 3 days or frozen up to 6 months.

Beef Broth

1 pound beef soup bones (ask your butcher if the bones are not already wrapped up in the meat section), 1 small diced onion, 1 chopped carrot, 2 chopped celery stalks, 2 cloves of garlic, 1 bouquet garni*

Chicken Broth

Carcass/bones from 1 whole chicken, 1 small diced onion, 2 chopped carrots, 1 chopped celery stalk, 2–3 cloves of garlic, 1 bouquet garni*, 8 peppercorns

Mushroom Broth

1 small diced onion, 1 celery stalk, 2 cups mushrooms (any variety), 2 bay leaves, 2 sprigs of oregano

Turkey Broth

Don't forget to save those turkey bones around the holidays! Turkey broth is a once-a-year treat that my family enjoys. Prepare as you would the chicken broth. I also like to throw in a few sage leaves.

Veggie Broth

1 small diced onion, 2 chopped carrots, 2 chopped celery stalks, 3–4 cloves of garlic, 1 bouquet garni*

***What is a bouquet garni?** A bouquet garni is a gathering or bouquet of fresh herbs. Traditionally it is a combination of thyme, parsley, and a bay leaf, but you make it whatever your taste buds call for! There are many ways to gather the herbs. You can simply tie a piece of twine around the bundle. Some people prefer to tie it up in a piece of cheesecloth and then secure the top with a piece of string or twine. There is always the option to purchase a bouquet garni already assembled as some specialty stores have them prepared for you in the spice section.*

Slow Cooker Beef Bone Broth

Bone broth is different than traditional broths because you cook it longer to really pull out the minerals and collagen from the bones. You can purchase beef bones from most butchers. If the bones are not prepackaged, just ask. Homemade bone broth is a popular item these days, and you are not the first to ask for these bones. Your butcher will know exactly what you want.

What do you do with bone broth?

Bone broth can be sipped right out of the cup on its own. Heck, it is even served at many trendy restaurants these days. It will come out of the refrigerator in a gelatinous state, but watch it melt as you heat some up and enjoy the restorative qualities. You can also use bone broth in simple broth-based soups, starters for sauces, or when steaming vegetables.

Can I add other flavors to my bone broth?

Absolutely! Change up the herbs for your different moods or even add a knob of ginger to the pot if your tummy needs some mending. Exclude the garlic if you are not a fan. The important parts of this recipe are the bones, the vinegar (it helps extract minerals from the bones), the water, and the slow-low cooking. After that, it is your baby.

ingredients

3 pounds beef soup bones

1 medium carrot, chopped

2 celery stalks, chopped

1 large onion, chopped

4 cloves of garlic, peeled and quartered

1 tablespoon black peppercorns

1 bouquet garni of preferred herbs

2 tablespoons apple cider vinegar

1 teaspoon sea salt *(I prefer to keep the salt on the light side so I can properly adjust it when using the broth in other recipes)*

directions

Place ingredients in a 6-quart slow cooker. Fill slow cooker with water to just cover the ingredients. Cook covered on low overnight for up to 12 hours, or even more if time permits.

Strain liquid through a colander to remove bones and larger pieces. Strain again through a sieve or cheesecloth to remove additional smaller pieces. Refrigerate.

You should have a very white solid layer of fat at the top of your broth. Remove this with the edge of a large spoon and discard (although some people like the additional fat, so again, this is really your personal preference). You will be left with a gelatinous pot of a yummy superfood underneath.

Store broth in an airtight container in the refrigerator for approximately 3–4 days or in the freezer for up to a year.

creamy soups — quick and simple

creamy soups — quick and simple

Creamy Broccoli Soup

ingredients

2 tablespoons ghee or real butter

1 medium onion, diced

1 celery stalk, diced

1 medium head broccoli, chopped

4 cups veggie or chicken broth

1 tablespoon dried thyme

Sea salt and ground pepper, to taste

directions

In a soup pot over medium heat, sauté ghee, onion, and celery until veggies are tender. Add broccoli, broth, and seasonings. Bring to a boil. Reduce heat to a simmer and continue to cook covered for 30 minutes. Using an immersion blender, blend until smooth. Taste and add additional salt and pepper if necessary. *Enjoy!*

Creamy Butternut Squash Soup

ingredients

2 tablespoons ghee or real butter

2 shallots, diced

1 celery stalk, diced

3 cups cubed butternut squash

4 cups veggie or chicken broth

1 tablespoon dried sage

Sea salt and ground pepper, to taste

directions

In a soup pot over medium heat, sauté ghee, shallots, and celery until veggies are tender. Add butternut squash, broth, and seasonings. Bring to a boil. Reduce heat to a simmer and continue to cook covered for 30 minutes. Using an immersion blender, blend until smooth. Taste and add additional salt and pepper if necessary. *Enjoy!*

Creamy Chicken Soup

ingredients

2 tablespoons ghee
or real butter

1 medium onion, diced

1 celery stalk, diced

3 cups diced uncooked chicken

4 cups chicken broth

1 tablespoon Italian seasoning

directions

In a soup pot over medium heat, sauté ghee, onion, and celery until veggies are tender. Add chicken, broth, and seasonings. Bring to a boil. Reduce heat to a simmer and continue to cook covered for 30 minutes. Using an immersion blender, blend until smooth. Taste and add additional salt and pepper if necessary. *Enjoy!*

Creamy Mushroom Soup

ingredients

3 tablespoons ghee
or real butter

1 medium onion, diced

1 celery stalk, diced

3 cups mushrooms of choice

4 cups mushroom
or chicken broth

1 tablespoon Italian seasoning

Sea salt and ground pepper,
to taste

directions

In a soup pot over medium heat, sauté ghee, onion, and celery until veggies are tender. Add mushrooms, broth, and seasonings. Bring to a boil. Reduce heat to a simmer and continue to cook covered for 30 minutes. Using an immersion blender, blend until smooth. Taste and add additional salt and pepper if necessary. *Enjoy!*

Creamy Tomato Soup

ingredients

2 tablespoons ghee
or real butter

1 medium carrot, diced

1 celery stalk, diced

28-ounce can crushed organic
tomatoes, with juice

3 cups veggie or chicken broth

1 tablespoon dried basil

Sea salt and ground pepper,
to taste

directions

In a soup pot over medium heat, sauté ghee, carrot, and celery until veggies are tender. Add tomatoes, broth, and seasonings. Bring to a boil. Reduce heat to a simmer and continue to cook covered for 30 minutes. Using an immersion blender, blend until smooth. Taste and add additional salt and pepper if necessary. *Enjoy!*

Cavegirl Tip: *Reduce the amount of broth to 2 cups and add 2 tablespoons of cassava flour or arrowroot starch to create homemade "condensed" soup bases for casserole recipes! The condensed soup will thicken as it cools.*

soup recipes

asian coconut chicken soup

When choosing a fish sauce, really read the ingredient label, as so many are filled with sugars and filler ingredients. My favorite choice is Red Boat fish sauce. I can't say it any better than them: "Red Boat is an all-natural, first press, 'extra virgin' Vietnamese fish sauce. It does not contain added water, preservatives or MSG. Made from a two hundred-year-old, chemical-free, artisanal process, Red Boat uses only the freshest cá com (black anchovy), salted minutes after leaving the sea then slow aged for over a year in traditional wooden barrels. Red Boat anchovies are sourced exclusively from the crystal clear waters off the Phu Quoc Island archipelago."

ingredients

13.5-ounce can of coconut milk

3 cups chicken broth

8 kaffir lime leaves (or zest of ½ lime)

10 thin circle slices of fresh ginger (about an inch knob)

2 stalks lemongrass, quartered (hard layer and ends removed)

1 tablespoon peppercorns of choice

2 tablespoons fish sauce

1 teaspoon sea salt

2 teaspoons tomato paste

1 large carrot, peeled and sliced into circles

2 scallions, sliced (ends removed)

2 cups (about 5 ounces) sliced shiitakes, or mushrooms of choice

1 pound chicken thighs, diced into 1-inch pieces

¼ cup chopped cilantro (and extra for garnish)

1 lime, quartered

Chili threads or chili oil for garnish*

directions

Place coconut milk, chicken broth, lime leaves, ginger, lemongrass, peppercorns, fish sauce, sea salt, and tomato paste in a large saucepan. Bring to a boil. Reduce heat and simmer for 20 minutes.

Strain coconut milk mixture. Discard the solids and add the liquid back to the saucepan.

Add carrots, mushrooms, chicken, and cilantro. Bring to a boil. Reduce heat and simmer for 10 minutes until chicken is tender and cooked through. Taste broth. Season with additional salt, if necessary.

Garnish each bowl with a lime quarter, chili threads, and fresh cilantro leaves. *Enjoy!*

**Substitute a serrano or jalapeño if you don't have either chili threads or chili oil. The soup needs a little heat!*

Cavegirl Tip: *Kaffir lime leaves are used in the same way that bay leaves are used. They lend a flavor to your soup but are then discarded before serving. Specialty stores and Asian markets carry them in the spice section; however, they can also be ordered online.*

bacon chicken chowder

Bacon. Do I need to go any further? This is just a good ole' family favorite that is inexpensive, easy to make, and just plain tastes good. The flavors and ingredients are completely accessible.

ingredients

6 slices of bacon

1 large onion, diced

1 celery stalk, diced

1 medium carrot, peeled and diced

1 parsnip, peeled and diced

4 cups chicken broth

½ teaspoon sea salt

1 teaspoon ground pepper

1 pound chicken breasts, diced into 1-inch squares

2 tablespoons fresh oregano leaves

1 tablespoon fresh thyme leaves, plus some for garnish

directions

In a soup pot or Dutch oven, cook bacon until crisp. Set bacon aside on a paper towel-lined plate.

Remove all but one tablespoon of bacon grease from bottom of pot. Add onion, celery, carrot, and parsnip. Sauté over medium heat until onions are translucent, scraping brown bits off the bottom.

Add broth, salt, pepper and 4 slices of crumbled bacon (reserving the other two slices for garnish). Bring to a boil. Reduce heat and simmer covered for 20 minutes. Add chicken, oregano, and thyme. Continue to cook for approximately 10 minutes until chicken is tender and cooked through. Taste broth. Add additional salt and pepper if necessary.

Divide soup into 4–6 bowls. Garnish with additional crumbled bacon and thyme leaves. *Enjoy!*

Cavegirl Tip: *If using dried instead of fresh herbs in this recipe, use 2 teaspoons of dried oregano and 1 teaspoon of dried thyme. When adding them to the broth, pinch or rub them between your fingers to release some of their "life" and potency.*

brats and beer stew

Did someone say football season?! Depending on the size of your game-day party, double or triple this recipe. It is tasty, comforting…and well, it's just good dude food! And, believe me, no will ever know that you used gluten-free beer! Even serve some brew stew-side while watching the big screen. Oh, and humor me: This one is for my dad…Go DAWGS, Sic 'Em…woof, woof!!

ingredients

3 slices bacon, diced

1 large onion, diced

3 celery stalks, sliced

2 large carrots, peeled and diced

2 12-ounce gluten-free beers

1 cup beef broth

1 pound uncooked bratwurst in casings

2 cups diced potatoes (gold or sweet)

14.5-ounce can diced tomatoes (fire-roasted, if you can get your hands on some)

1 teaspoon balsamic vinegar

1 teaspoon Sriracha, or preferred hot sauce

directions

In a soup pot or Dutch oven, heat bacon over medium until almost crispy, just to render the fat. Add onion, celery, and carrots. Continue to sauté for an additional minute or two. Add beer and broth scraping the browned bits off bottom of pot.

Poke each bratwurst with a fork one or two times. Add to pot. Bring to a boil. Reduce and simmer covered for 10 minutes. Remove bratwurst from pot and slice into 1-inch pieces. Add back to pot.

Add potatoes, diced tomatoes, vinegar, and hot sauce. Bring to a boil. Reduce heat and simmer for 30 minutes until potatoes are tender. Taste broth. Add salt if necessary. *Enjoy!*

Cavegirl Tip: *Some folks take exception to Sriracha because it is not pure and has some unfortunate ingredients. I happen to allow this beautiful hot sauce into my life because I make my own. Michelle Tam and Henry Fong from Nom Nom Paleo have a nomtastic recipe on their site.*

cavegirl pho

Although Pho is a traditional Vietnamese noodle soup, I think this Cavegirl version hits all of the flavor notes that you may be seeking. There is a little sweet...a little sour...a little heat...and a lot of fresh!

ingredients

1 tablespoon avocado oil, or preferred cooking oil

½ medium yellow onion, diced

3 star anise pods

4–5 cloves of garlic, slightly crushed (but cloves still intact)

3-inch knob of ginger, peeled

1 cinnamon stick

3 cups beef broth

1 cup water

2 cups shiitake mushrooms (or mushrooms of choice), sliced

2 tablespoons of fish sauce (Red Boat is the Paleo approved brand)

1 pound boneless ribeye steak, or preferred cut

1 medium turnip, peeled

2–3 scallions, thinly sliced (plus some of the green portion)

Handful of fresh Thai basil leaves (or basil)

Handful of fresh mint leaves

Handful of fresh cilantro leaves

1 serrano pepper, thinly sliced (seed it if you don't want as much heat)

1 lime, cut into 6 segments

directions

In a soup pot or Dutch oven, heat oil on medium-high heat. Add onion, star anise, garlic, ginger, and cinnamon stick. Sauté for about 4 minutes until onions are translucent.

Add broth and water. Bring to a boil. Cover and reduce heat. Simmer for 30 minutes.

While broth simmers, do the knife work. Remove herb leaves from stems. Slice mushrooms, pepper, and scallions. THINLY slice your beef. Spiral cut or julienne the turnip. Set everything aside and have it ready to roll.

Using a slotted spoon, remove onion, star anise, garlic, ginger, and cinnamon stick from broth. Discard. Add mushrooms and fish sauce. Bring up to medium-high heat and cook for 5 minutes. Add beef and turnip. Cook for an additional 2–3 minutes (depending on your preference for the doneness of the meat). Season with salt to taste.

Divide soup into four bowls. Serve immediately with remaining ingredients (herbs, limes, onions, peppers) on the side for everyone to choose their soup additions. *Enjoy!*

chicken and dumplings

I have found a way for you to have your dumplings and eat them, too! Unfortunately (or fortunately!), these are not like the traditional drop dumplings. Without the elastic gluten, these would just disintegrate in the broth. With that said, once baked and added to your bowl of soup, you get the mouthfeel of a dumpling adding another level of comfort to this bowl of goodness.

ingredients

Chicken Stew:

3 pounds chicken thighs (about 6)

4 tablespoons ghee or real butter

2 tablespoons cassava flour

3–4 medium carrots, peeled and chopped

3 celery stalks, chopped

1 onion, diced

1 parsnip, peeled and diced

2–3 cloves of garlic, minced

3 cups chicken broth

4 teaspoons thyme leaves

Dumplings:

1 large sweet potato, peeled and diced

½ cup cassava flour

⅓ cup coconut flour

2 large eggs

2 tablespoons ghee or real butter

½ teaspoon fine sea salt

2 teaspoons Italian seasoning

1 teaspoon baking powder

directions

Preheat oven to 350 degrees Fahrenheit.

Place chicken thighs in a lightly greased baking dish. Cook for 30 minutes. Set aside and let cool. Dice when cooled.

In a medium saucepan, start boiling sweet potatoes. Reduce to medium heat and cook until they are fork tender. Drain and set aside.

In a soup pot or Dutch oven, melt ghee with carrots, celery, onion, turnip, and arrowroot. Sauté until onions are translucent. Add garlic and give the ingredients a toss. Add chicken broth, thyme, and chicken. Let simmer for 45 minutes.

Blend sweet potatoes along with additional dumpling ingredients until smooth. Batter should be sticky, but not runny. Add a little extra cassava flour if needed. On a parchment paper-lined baking sheet, place 2-teaspoon sized balls of dumpling mixture. Bake for 30–35 minutes until outside is a little crispy. Let cool.

Spoon chicken stew into bowls. Throw a couple of dumplings into each bowl and put any remaining dumplings in the middle of the table...they'll get eaten! Garnish with thyme leaves. *Enjoy!*

chicken, shrimp, and andouille sausage gumbo

My family and I recently took a trip to New Orleans, and to say that the food there is good is such an understatement. Also, no two gumbos seem to be alike. So make this recipe with a heart full of love and don't get caught up in exacts. Taste it as you go and add flavor where you think necessary...and enjoy it with a group of happy people around your table.

ingredients

3 tablespoons ghee or real butter

¼ cup cassava flour or arrowroot flour

1 medium onion, diced

2 large carrots, peeled and sliced

3 celery stalks, sliced

3 cups chicken broth

8 ounces clam juice

1 pound uncooked andouille sausage, in casings

1 pound medium shrimp, peeled and deveined

1 pound chicken breast, diced

12 ounces frozen okra, sliced

2 teaspoons gumbo file (or creole seasoning)

directions

In a soup pot or Dutch oven over medium heat, melt ghee. Slowly whisk in flour and continue to stir until this "roux" turns brownish. Add onion, carrots, and celery. Sauté until onions are tender. Whisk in chicken broth. Add clam juice.

Bring mixture to a boil. Reduce heat to a simmer. Add andouille sausage and simmer covered for 10 minutes. Using a slotted spoon, remove sausage to a cutting board. Cut into 1-inch pieces. Add back to soup pot. Add shrimp, chicken, and okra. Continue to simmer covered for 30 minutes. Stir in gumbo file. Taste and add salt if necessary. *Enjoy!*

chorizo-chicken chiloup

I started out thinking that this recipe would be a soup, but then it had a little bit of a resemblance to a chili, or maybe a stew...so I asked my trusted Facebook folks, and they advised calling it a Chiloup, Stilli, Stewli, Schillew, and even a Stoup! So, take your pick, but definitely give this tasty version of Paleo chili a try!

ingredients

1 pound chorizo, loose or removed from casings

1 red onion, diced

1 small red bell pepper, or color of choice, seeded and diced

8 ounces baby bella mushrooms, or mushrooms of choice, sliced

2 tablespoons ghee or real butter

3 celery stalks, chopped

3 carrots, peeled and chopped

½ teaspoon ground coriander

½ teaspoon smoked paprika

Sea salt and ground pepper, to taste

1 pound chicken thighs, uncooked and small diced

4 cups chicken or veggie broth

28-ounce can of diced tomatoes, strained

Optional Garnishes:
Sliced black olives, fresh cilantro, diced avocado

directions

In a soup pot or Dutch oven over medium heat, cook chorizo, onion, bell pepper, and mushrooms until chorizo is browned. Add ghee, celery, carrots, coriander, paprika, salt, and pepper. Sauté for 5 minutes. Add chicken, broth, and diced tomatoes.

Cook covered on medium-low for 30 minutes.

Continue to simmer uncovered for one hour. Spoon chili into bowls and garnish with optional toppings. *Enjoy!*

clean out the crisper celery soup

If your kitchen habits are like mine, then there are several weeks out of the year with rotting celery in the bottom of your crisper. Good intentions, ya know? This recipe solves the crisper problem, and the result is a very fresh and homestyle creamy soup!

ingredients

2 pieces bacon, chopped

2 tablespoons ghee
or real butter

10 celery stalks, chopped (save celery leaves for garnish), diced

1 yellow bell pepper, or color of choice, seeded and diced

½ head cauliflower, chopped

¼ teaspoon smoked paprika

⅛ teaspoon cayenne pepper

Handful of fresh parsley leaves

2–3 cloves of garlic

4 cups veggie or chicken broth

Sea salt and ground pepper,
to taste

Optional Garnishes:
Chopped leaves from the celery, edible flowers

directions

In a soup pot or Dutch oven, place bacon and ghee over medium heat. Add celery, bell pepper, cauliflower, paprika, cayenne, parsley, and garlic. Sauté for about 5 minutes until celery starts to tender.

Add broth. Bring to a boil. Cover and reduce to a simmer for 30 minutes. Taste. Add salt and pepper to taste. Using an immersion blender, blend until smooth. Alternately, use a stand mixer with batches of the mixture to blend.

Garnish with celery leaves and/or edible flowers. *Enjoy!*

cowboy beef stew

Take off your cowboy hat and mosey over to the table...it's supper time! Don't skip the coffee in this rub. It lends richness and another level of flavor to this hearty dude food that is sure to please even the pickiest of Paleo followers.

ingredients

Cowboy Dry Rub:

1 teaspoon instant coffee crystals

1 teaspoon smoked paprika

½ teaspoon onion powder

½ teaspoon ground cumin

½ teaspoon cayenne pepper

½ teaspoon ground mustard

½ teaspoon garlic powder

½ teaspoon sea salt

¼ teaspoon ground coriander

Stew Ingredients:

1.5 pounds beef stew cubes

2 tablespoons avocado oil, or cooking oil of choice

1 yellow onion, chopped

3 celery stalks, chopped

1 red bell pepper, seeded and diced

1 small turnip, peeled and small diced

4 cups beef broth

1 teaspoon garlic powder

1 teaspoon chili powder

1 teaspoon sea salt

1 teaspoon ground pepper

1 jalapeño, seeded and diced

Sea salt and ground pepper, to taste

Optional Garnish:

Chopped cilantro or parsley leaves

directions

Combine *Cowboy Rub* ingredients and massage into beef stew cubes. In a storage bowl, combine rub and beef stew cubes. Refrigerate for 1 hour up to overnight.

In a soup pot or Dutch oven, heat oil. Sear all sides of beef in batches, maybe a minute per side (do your best on this one — it is not an exact science). Set aside.

Add onions, celery, bell pepper, and turnip to pot. Sauté for a couple of minutes. Add ½ cup of beef broth. Stir, making sure you scrape those brown bits off bottom of pot. Add garlic powder, chili powder, salt, pepper, and jalapeño.

Add remaining broth. Bring to a boil. Reduce heat to a simmer uncovered for one hour. Taste and add additional salt and pepper if necessary.

Serve immediately. Garnish with chopped cilantro or parsley. *Enjoy!*

creamy ham and bok choy soup

Switch out that familiar green cabbage for some bok choy, also known as Chinese white cabbage. This cruciferous veggie is a nutritional powerhouse packed with fiber, vitamins, and minerals. Fighting inflammation, lowering blood pressure, improving immunity, and promoting skin health, this fresh Chinese native is a great new substitution to your familiar traditional recipes.

ingredients

2 tablespoons ghee or real butter

1 large parsnip, peeled and chopped

1 large sweet onion, chopped

1 tablespoon Italian seasoning

¼ teaspoon sea salt

¼ teaspoon ground pepper

1 pound smoked ham, cubed

4 cups chicken broth

Pinch of red pepper flakes

3 cups bok choy, chopped

Garnish:

Chopped green leafy part of bok choy

directions

In a soup pot or Dutch oven, heat ghee on medium heat. Add parsnip, onion, Italian seasoning, salt, pepper, and a quarter of the ham. Sauté until onions are translucent.

Add three cups of chicken broth. Bring to a boil. Reduce heat and simmer in a lidded pot for 30 minutes until parsnips are fork tender. Using an immersion blender, blend until smooth (or use a stand blender with batches of the soup).

Stir in bok choy and remaining ham and chicken broth. Taste and adjust salt level to your liking. Bring to a boil. Reduce heat and simmer covered for an additional 30 minutes.

Ladle into bowls and garnish with chopped bok choy leaves. *Enjoy!*

curried roasted carrot and tomato soup

Not only do the carrots bring sweetness to this classic soup, but roasting the vegetables also creates caramelization which brings out the natural sugars. Don't worry about seeding your tomatoes; everything will get pureed so the more, the better.

ingredients

2 pounds tomatoes, any variety, halved (I used a mix of Romas, Beefsteak, & Yellow Pear varieties from my garden)

4 small carrots, peeled and quartered

¼ head of cauliflower, broken into florets

1 large Vidalia onion or sweet variety of choice

4–5 cloves of garlic

Avocado oil, or preferred oil, for drizzling

Sea salt and ground pepper, to taste

2 tablespoons ghee or real butter

2 celery stalks, chopped

4 cups chicken or veggie broth

5 large basil leaves

1 teaspoon sea salt (or more if desired)

2 teaspoons curry powder

1 tablespoon cooking Sherry

Optional Garnishes:

Cooked, crumbled bacon and additional basil

directions

Preheat oven to 400 degrees Fahrenheit.

In two large baking dishes lined with parchment paper, scatter the tomatoes, carrots, cauliflower, onion, and garlic cloves. Drizzle lightly with oil. Give it a quick toss. Season with salt and pepper. Bake for 30 minutes.

While veggies bake, place ghee and celery in a soup pot or Dutch oven over medium-high heat. Sauté for about 4 minutes. Add roasted veggies, broth, basil leaves, salt, curry powder, and Sherry. Bring to a boil. Cover and reduce to a simmer for 30 minutes.

Using an immersion blender (or you can use a stand blender alternating batches of the soup), blend until smooth. Either serve immediately or let simmer covered for an additional half hour to let the flavors marry together.

Garnish with optional bacon crumbles and basil (cut chiffonade). *Enjoy!*

Cavegirl Tip: *If you've never used parchment paper, go buy a roll right now. You don't need to use oil because parchment paper is non-stick, clean-up is great because the paper is disposable, and you lengthen the life of your pans!*

duck and butternut squash stew

I first got the idea for this recipe from a duck salsa I had at a beautiful little restaurant called Asiatique in Louisville, Kentucky. It was a flavor explosion and the duck fit perfectly. I would have never put duck and jalapeño together, but once my mind started going, I thought a stew would be the perfect venue for these flavors. If you don't have duck available, the dark meat of chicken thighs is a great substitute and should blend nicely.

ingredients

2 tablespoons ghee or real butter

1 leek, chopped

2 cups turnip, peeled and diced (about 1 medium turnip)

3–4 cloves of garlic

4 cups chicken broth

1 tablespoon coconut oil

3 duck breasts, fat layer removed and discarded, duck meat diced

2 cups butternut squash, small-diced

2 cups shiitake mushrooms, sliced

½ cup bell pepper (approximately 1 small), color of choice, diced

2 carrots, peeled and diced

1 teaspoon orange zest

1 small jalapeño, seeded and diced

1 tablespoon cooking Sherry

1 tablespoon fresh thyme leaves

1 tablespoon chopped fresh rosemary

Optional toppings:
Thinly sliced jalapeños and/or finely-chopped rosemary

directions

In a saucepan, heat ghee over medium heat. Add leeks and turnips. Cook until leeks are translucent. Add garlic cloves and 2 cups of chicken broth. Bring to a boil. Reduce heat to a simmer. Cook until turnips are tender. In the meantime, go to step 2.

In a soup pot or Dutch oven, add coconut oil and diced duck over medium heat. Cook for 1 minute while stirring. Add remaining 2 cups of chicken broth, butternut squash, mushrooms, bell pepper, carrots, orange zest, jalapeño, Sherry, thyme, and rosemary. Season with salt and pepper. Bring to a boil. Reduce heat and simmer for 45 minutes.

Using an immersion blender, blend until smooth. Alternately, use a stand mixer with batches of mixture to blend.

Add saucepan ingredients to Dutch oven ingredients. Stir.

Taste. Season with additional salt and pepper if necessary. Ladle into bowls. Garnish with sliced jalapeños and/or rosemary. *Enjoy!*

easy chicken thigh curry

I suppose this isn't a soup exactly, but it does contain broth, and it is dang good. This is great served over riced cauliflower. Just take a head of cauliflower and grate it. Bingo. You have riced cauliflower. Toss it in a skillet over medium heat with a little salt and pepper until warmed. Spoon the "rice" into the bottom of each bowl. Ladle your curry over the top and enjoy!

ingredients

1 tablespoon curry powder

2 teaspoons garam masala

1 teaspoon sea salt

½ teaspoon chili powder

½ teaspoon fennel seeds

2 pounds chicken thighs, cubed

1 large onion, diced

1 tablespoon ghee or real butter

1 jalapeño, seeded and small diced

1 medium turnip, peeled and small diced

1 teaspoon ginger, minced

3–4 garlic cloves, minced

8 ounces chicken broth

¼ cup coconut milk (the solid part at the top of the can)

2 tablespoons tomato paste

¼ cup chopped fresh basil leaves, plus additional for garnish

directions

In a large bowl, mix curry powder, garam masala, salt, chili powder, and fennel seeds.

Add chicken to seasonings and toss. I use my hands, but that is an optional step.

In a soup pot or Dutch oven, heat ghee over medium-high heat. Add chicken, onion, jalapeño, and turnip. Cook for 10 minutes, stirring several times to make sure chicken pieces are seared.

Add ginger, garlic, broth, coconut milk, and tomato paste. Stir to blend. Bring to a boil. Reduce and let simmer uncovered for 30 minutes.

In the last 5 minutes of cooking, add chopped basil. Serve in bowls and garnish with additional chopped basil. *Enjoy!*

garden veggie soup

If you are looking for a lighter but completely satisfying meal, this soup delivers. Chock full of nutrients and fibrous, filling veggies, enjoy this hearty bowl as a meal or as a starter.

ingredients

3 tablespoons ghee, real butter, or preferred cooking oil

1 medium onion, diced

2 celery stalks, diced

2 medium carrots, peeled and diced

5 cups veggie broth (or broth of choice)

1 turnip, peeled and diced

2 cups cabbage, chopped

4–5 garlic cloves, minced

1 tablespoon thyme leaves plus extra for garnish

1 teaspoon sea salt

1 teaspoon ground pepper

directions

In a soup pot or Dutch oven over medium heat, sauté ghee, onion, celery, and carrots until onions are translucent.

Add broth, turnip, cabbage, garlic, thyme, salt, and pepper.

Bring to a boil. Reduce heat and let simmer for 40 minutes. Taste. Add more salt and pepper if needed. Garnish with additional thyme. *Enjoy!*

garlic kale soup with a poached egg

This is an amazingly easy soup to cook and perfect when you are feeling a little under the weather. The poached egg lends creaminess to a traditional broth-based recipe. This soup will be sure to get you back on your feet again!

ingredients

1 tablespoon avocado oil, or preferred cooking oil

2 shallots, peeled and diced

½ cup turnip, peeled and diced

4–6 cloves of garlic, peeled and small diced

1 small carrot, long thin peels (use a veggie peeler)

4 cups chicken broth

1 cup cooked chicken (breast or thigh), diced

1 packed cup of kale, chopped

1 bouquet garni

4 poached eggs

directions

In a soup pot or Dutch oven, heat oil, shallots, and turnips on medium heat until shallots are translucent. Add garlic and carrots. Stir. Add broth, chicken, and kale.

Bring ingredients to a boil. Cover and reduce to a simmer for 30 minutes.

While soup simmers, poach eggs in the last 10 minutes.

Serve immediately in four bowls. Garnish with a poached egg. *Enjoy!*

good ole' southern potlikker soup

Growing up in the South, we always ate Hoppin' John, a dish made with black-eyed peas and rice on a bed of greens, for New Year's Day. It was supposed to bring you luck and, well, it is just tasty. After adopting the Paleo lifestyle, this meal wasn't an option anymore because of the beans and rice. So I did some research and found a beautiful traditional potlikker soup. It also contains greens, which means I'll be financially set for the year... right? I'll keep thinking that and enjoying my new Good Ole' Southern Potlikker Soup!

ingredients

3 tablespoons ghee or real butter

1 large onion, diced

1 pound (approximately) uncured, fully-cooked ham steak, cubed

2–3 garlic cloves, minced

2 celery stalks, chopped

2 medium carrots, peeled and chopped

6 cups chicken or veggie broth

4 cups kale, chopped (well rinsed and middle vein and stems discarded)

6 cups collards, chopped (well rinsed and middle vein and stems discarded) *Note: mustard or turnip greens can be used also*

1 tablespoon apple cider vinegar

1 tablespoon Sriracha, or preferred hot sauce

Sea salt and ground pepper, to taste

directions

In a soup pot or Dutch oven, heat ghee, onion, ham, garlic, celery, and carrots.

Cook over medium heat and stir until onions are translucent.

Add broth, scraping any bits off bottom of pot. Add greens, apple cider vinegar, Sriracha, salt, and pepper.

Bring to a boil. Reduce heat and cover. Simmer for 1.5 hours. Taste and add more salt and/or pepper if necessary. *Enjoy!*

hamburger soup

Skip the drive-thru and make this inexpensive and very tasty recipe. This quick soup evokes all of the flavors of a hamburger, but don't skip the dill pickle garnish. As weird as it may sound, it really pulls all of the flavors together.

ingredients

1 pound ground beef

1 medium onion, diced

1 bell pepper (color of choice), seeded and diced

2 cups cherry tomatoes

1 teaspoon ground mustard

1 teaspoon smoked paprika

1 teaspoon garlic powder

½ teaspoon sea salt

2 bay leaves

4 cups beef broth

2 handfuls iceberg lettuce, shredded

½ cup dill pickles, diced

directions

In a soup pot or Dutch oven, heat ground beef, onion, and bell pepper over medium heat until ground beef is no longer pink. Tip pot and spoon out any excess liquid. Discard.

Add cherry tomatoes. You can cut them in half, but I just pop them with my fingers one at a time into the pot. Add ground mustard, smoked paprika, garlic powder, salt, and bay leaves. Stir.

Add beef broth. Bring to a boil. Reduce heat and simmer covered for 30 minutes.

Remove bay leaves and discard. Stir in shredded lettuce and continue to cook for 10 minutes. Spoon soup into bowls and garnish with dill pickles. *Enjoy!*

BONUS! *TWO Cavegirl Tips:* *1. Iceberg lettuce can generally be found in the salad section of most grocers already shredded. 2. With the dill pickles, read your labels — they are not all created equal. Keep your eye on the sugar grams.*

homestyle venison stew

If you are a hunter, or if you have a generous hunter friend, this venison stew is a great use of the meat. Because deer meat can't be regulated, you won't see it in the local grocery store. So, if you can't get your hands on some venison, substitute a beef or bison roast and be equally as happy!

ingredients

3–4 pound venison roast (or beef roast)

2 tablespoons ghee, bacon grease, or oil or choice

2 medium carrots, peeled and diced

2 celery stalks, chopped into crescents

1 medium sweet onion, diced

1 medium turnip, peeled and diced

2 tablespoons fresh thyme leaves, plus extra for optional garnish

1 tablespoon Worcestershire sauce

Sea salt and ground pepper, to taste

3 cups beef broth, or broth of choice

28-ounce can organic crushed tomatoes

directions

Place roast in a slow cooker. Cover with water. Cook on lowest setting overnight.

In the morning, cut roast into ½-inch cubes.

In a soup pot or Dutch oven, heat ghee, carrots, celery, onion, and turnip over medium heat until onions are tender. Add cubed meat. Cook for an additional 3 minutes. Add thyme, Worcestershire sauce, salt, pepper, broth, and crushed tomatoes. Stir.

Bring to a boil. Reduce heat to a simmer. Cover and simmer for 1 hour. Serve. Garnish with additional thyme leaves, if desired. *Enjoy!*

island seafood chowder

Are you missing the island, mon? Well, slap a soup pot on the stove, and in less than a few hours, you will be at the beach again. Grab a few gluten-free beers, invite some friends over, prop your feet up, and enjoy this taste of the ocean!

ingredients

Creamy Soup Base:

4 tablespoons real butter or ghee

2 celery stalks, chopped

1 small onion, diced

1 medium carrot, peeled and diced

1 small parsnip, peeled and diced

4 Roma tomatoes, seeded and diced

2 teaspoons jerk spice

4 cups chicken broth

Chowder:

1 cup canned coconut milk

1 large parsnip, peeled and diced

1 pound medium shrimp, peeled and deveined

½ pound calamari tubes, cut into rings

¾ pound halibut, cut into 1-inch cubes

1 bunch asparagus, hard ends cut off and remaining cut into 1-inch sections

1 teaspoon red pepper flakes

1 teaspoon garlic powder

1 tablespoon cooking Sherry

Sea salt and ground pepper, to taste

Optional Garnishes:

Crumbled bacon and freshly ground pepper

directions

In a soup pot or Dutch oven, place butter, celery, onion, carrot, small parsnip, tomatoes, and jerk spice. Cook on medium for approximately 5 minutes until onions are translucent.

Add chicken broth. Bring to a boil and then reduce heat. Simmer until parsnips are fork tender. Using an immersion blender, blend until smooth. (Alternative: use a stand blender to puree in batches and return to pot).

Whisk in the coconut milk. Add the large parsnip, shrimp, calamari, halibut, asparagus, red pepper flakes, garlic powder, coconut milk, salt, and pepper.

Cook on medium-low for about 30 minutes to really let flavors blend together.

Ladle soup into bowls and garnish with crumbled bacon and ground pepper if desired. *Enjoy!*

italian sausage soup

Mama mia! This is good soup! As a child of the 70's, my mother used to make a meal that had ground beef, zucchini, and stewed tomatoes served over a bed of rice. Remember that one? If so, you also had to be home when the street lights came on, and you agree that disco is still alive. If not, know that this is a great, clean soup version of that delicious classic!

ingredients

1 pound Italian sausage (loose or removed from casings)

1 medium onion, diced

1 bell pepper (color of choice), seeded and diced

2 celery stalks, diced

1 teaspoon garlic powder

1 teaspoon sea salt

1 teaspoon ground pepper

14.5-ounce can diced tomatoes, liquid included

2 cups beef broth

1 large zucchini, diced

1 handful of baby kale

directions

In a soup pot or Dutch oven over medium-high heat, cook sausage, onion, bell pepper, celery, garlic powder, salt, and pepper until the sausage is cooked through.

Add tomatoes, broth, and zucchini. Bring to a boil. Reduce heat and simmer covered for 25 minutes. Add kale. Simmer for an additional five minutes. Before serving, taste and season with additional salt and pepper if necessary. *Enjoy!*

lobster (or crab) bisque

Lobster. Lobster. Lobster! This is one of the fan-favorites on my blog, cavegirlcuisine.com. Bisques are traditionally thickened with cream, but this version gives you all of the decadence without the yucky tummy upset from the dairy. I dare your guests to say a word about this one being Paleo. It is just a beautiful bowl of layered flavors with upscale lobster charm.

ingredients

1 pound lobster meat
(about 5 small lobster tails)

3.5 tablespoons ghee
or real butter

2 cups leeks, chopped
(approximately 2 large)

2 celery stalks, chopped

2 medium carrots,
peeled and large diced

½ head cauliflower,
roughly chopped

4 cups vegetable broth

2 cups water

1 tablespoon Herbes de
Provence (or Italian seasoning)

Sea salt and ground pepper,
to taste

1 bay leaf

4–6 garlic cloves,
peeled and whole

2 tablespoons cooking Sherry

6-ounce can tomato paste

Fresh thyme leaves, to garnish

directions

Fill a medium saucepan halfway with salted water. Bring to a boil. Carefully drop in lobster tails. Cook for 5 minutes. Remove tails from water. Let cool. Remove meat from shells. Set meat aside and roughly chop. Set large carcass parts/shells aside.

In a soup pot or Dutch oven, place 2 tablespoons ghee, leeks, celery, and carrots. Heat and cook until leeks are tender. Add broth, water, cauliflower, Herbes de Provence, salt, pepper, bay leaf, garlic cloves, and lobster shells. Bring to a boil. Reduce and simmer covered for 30 minutes.

Using a slotted spoon, remove shells and bay leaf. Discard.

Using an immersion blender, blend ingredients until smooth. (An alternative is to transfer small batches to a stand blender, and blend until smooth).

Add approximately ¾ of lobster meat back to pot along with cooking Sherry and tomato paste. Stir until combined and simmer.

In a small pan over medium heat, melt remaining ghee and add remaining lobster. Cook for 2 minutes until lobster meat is coated. Pour lobster bisque into bowls. Add a portion of buttered lobster to the center of the bowls and garnish with fresh thyme leaves. *Enjoy!*

Cavegirl Tip: *Substitute crab for an equally yummy recipe!*

manhattan clam chowder

White clam chowder, red clam chowder…well, this one is the red one! Both are fantastic, but we are concentrating on the latter today. So many layers of flavors…enjoy!

ingredients

4 pieces bacon, diced

1 medium onion, diced

3 celery stalks, diced

1 red bell pepper, or color of choice, seeded and diced

28-ounce can whole tomatoes, including juice

1.5 cups peeled and diced parsnips (about 2 medium)

1 tablespoon fresh thyme leaves, plus extra for garnish

1 tablespoon fresh parsley, chopped

1 tablespoon fresh oregano

½ teaspoon crushed red pepper flakes

1 bay leaf

1 teaspoon sea salt

1 teaspoon ground pepper

10-ounce can whole baby clams, including juice

4–5 garlic cloves, minced

2 cups veggie or chicken broth

1 large carrot, peeled and grated

directions

In a soup pot or Dutch oven over medium-high heat, cook bacon for 2 minutes. Add onion, celery, and bell pepper. Sauté until onions are translucent.

Add tomatoes, parsnips, thyme, parsley, oregano, red pepper flakes, bay leaf, salt, and pepper. Stir and cook for another 5 minutes, smooshing the tomatoes as it cooks.

Add clams, garlic, broth, and grated carrot.

Bring to a boil. Reduce heat. Simmer covered for 30 minutes until parsnips are fork tender. Taste broth. Add salt if necessary. Serve and garnish with fresh thyme leaves. *Enjoy!*

mexi-chorizo soup

Taco Tuesday does not have to include tortillas and crunchy taco shells. This below-the-border meal has all of the flavors of Mexico without the guilt. If spicy is your thing and the chorizo doesn't quite get it there for you, add some sliced jalapeño, either as a garnish or directly to the soup!

ingredients

1 pound chorizo,
loose or casings removed

1 small red onion, diced

2 Roma tomatoes,
seeded and diced

2 tomatillos,
husks removed and diced

4 cups beef broth

Juice from ½ lime

½ teaspoon sea salt

¼ cup cilantro leaves,
plus extra for garnish

1 avocado, sliced for garnish

directions

In a soup pot or Dutch oven over medium-high heat, add chorizo and onion. Sauté until chorizo is cooked through. Drain off any excess fat, and pat top of mixture with a couple of paper towels.

Add tomatoes, tomatillos, broth, lime juice, and salt. Bring to a boil. Reduce heat and continue to simmer covered for 20 minutes. Taste broth and add additional salt, if necessary. Add cilantro. Continue to simmer covered for 10 minutes.

Ladle soup into bowls. Garnish with cilantro and avocado slices (and jalapeño if you like additional heat). *Enjoy!*

minestrone (pasta-free and beanless)

Yes, the pasta and beans actually make it minestrone, but you get the point. This has all the flavor of traditional minestrone without the inflammatory qualities of grains and legumes!

ingredients

2 tablespoons ghee or real butter

1 large onion, diced

1 yellow bell pepper, seeded and diced

1 orange bell pepper, seeded and diced

1 large carrot, peeled and diced

2 celery stalks, diced

13.5-ounce can diced tomatoes

1 tablespoon Italian seasoning

½ teaspoon sea salt

1 teaspoon ground pepper

2–3 cloves of garlic, minced

3 cups veggie broth

2 tablespoons tomato paste

directions

In a soup pot or Dutch oven over medium heat, melt ghee. Add onion, bell pepper, carrot, and celery. Sauté until onions are translucent.

Add remaining ingredients. Bring to a boil. Reduce heat and simmer covered for 30 minutes. *Enjoy!*

n'awlins shrimp étouffée

I was originally going to make this recipe with crawfish, but my grocery store wasn't going to get their shipment for a couple of weeks, so shrimp it was! It is amazing how much depth of flavor you can achieve in such a short amount of time with this recipe. If you can get your hands on some fresh crawfish, use that for sure!

ingredients

5 tablespoons ghee or real butter

1 medium onion, diced

1 small green bell pepper, seeded and diced

2 celery stalks, diced

3 cloves of garlic, minced

1 pound medium shrimp, peeled and deveined

1.5 cups chicken or veggie broth

¼ cup cassava flour or arrowroot flour

1 tablespoon Creole seasoning

2 teaspoons preferred hot sauce

Sea salt and ground pepper, to taste

¼ cup chopped scallion tops

½ cup chopped parsley, stems removed

directions

In a 12-inch cast iron skillet, melt ghee over medium-high heat with onion, bell pepper, celery, and garlic. Sauté until onions are translucent. Add shrimp.

In a separate bowl, whisk together broth and cassava flour. Pour this mixture into the skillet. Add the Creole seasoning and hot sauce. Whisk in a pinch of salt and a few grinds of pepper.

Bring to a boil. Reduce heat. Add scallion tops and simmer until sauce is reduced and thickens. Taste and add salt or additional hot sauce if necessary.

Serve immediately. Garnish with chopped parsley. *Enjoy!*

oyster rockefeller soup

I bartended at a little oyster bar in Augusta, Georgia in my twenties while in college, and you would think that I'm over anything oyster. But, you'd be wrong. I love these little guys and their ability to take on the flavor wherever they grew up. You can eat oysters from all over the world and each grouping will have its own unique flavor. I hope you enjoy this Paleo version of a traditional oyster stew with a Rockefeller twist!

ingredients

4 tablespoons ghee or real butter

1 medium onion, diced

13.5-ounce can coconut milk

3–4 cloves of garlic, minced

½ teaspoon sea salt

1 teaspoon ground pepper

1 teaspoon fennel seeds

1 tablespoon Sriracha, or preferred hot sauce

3 cups chicken or veggie broth

6 ounces (about 2 handfuls) fresh spinach

2 dozen raw oysters, cleaned and shucked

Garnish – Fried Oysters:

1 dozen raw oysters, cleaned and shucked

¼ cup cassava flour

¼ cup arrowroot flour

½ teaspoon sea salt

½ teaspoon cayenne pepper

½ teaspoon ground pepper

2 large eggs

2 tablespoons avocado oil, bacon grease, or cooking oil of choice

directions

In a soup pot or Dutch oven over medium heat, melt ghee. Add onions and sauté until translucent. Stir in coconut milk, garlic, salt, pepper, fennel seeds, Sriracha, and broth. Bring to a boil and then reduce heat. Simmer covered for 15 minutes.

Add spinach and oysters to soup pot. Simmer covered for an additional 15 minutes.

While soup simmers, prepare fried oyster garnish. In a medium bowl, combine cassava flour, arrowroot flour, sea salt, cayenne pepper, and ground pepper. In a small bowl, whisk eggs. Set bowls aside.

In a large skillet, heat oil on high. Dip oysters in eggs and then dredge in flour mixture. Gently place oysters in skillet away from you so as not to splash hot oil in your direction. Cook several minutes per side until a golden brown color is achieved. Set fried oysters aside on a plate lined with a paper towel.

Ladle soup into bowls. Garnish top of soup with fried oysters. *Enjoy!*

pumpkin apple bacon soup

While the world is going pumpkin crazy, you can enjoy your very own recipe utilizing this carotene-rich food. It is a nice play on sweet and salty without going overboard on the concept.

ingredients

7 slices bacon

2 Granny Smith apples (or any tart variety), peeled, seeded, and diced

1 medium onion, diced

1 large carrot, peeled and diced

2 celery stalks, diced

15-ounce can pumpkin puree

3 cups veggie or chicken broth

¼ teaspoon garlic powder

¼ teaspoon smoked paprika

¼ teaspoon cinnamon

¼ teaspoon cayenne pepper

¼ teaspoon sea salt

directions

In a soup pot or Dutch oven, cook bacon until crisp. Set bacon aside on a paper towel-lined plate.

Remove all but one tablespoon of bacon grease from bottom of the pot. Add apples, onion, carrot, and celery. Cook over medium heat, scraping brown bits off bottom of pot, until onions are translucent.

Add pumpkin, broth, garlic powder, smoked paprika, cinnamon, cayenne pepper, salt, and 3 strips of chopped and cooked bacon. Bring to a boil. Reduce heat and simmer covered for 30 minutes.

Using an immersion blender, blend ingredients until smooth. (An alternative is to transfer small batches to a stand blender, and blend until smooth).

Ladle into four bowls. Add a chopped piece of bacon to each soup bowl as garnish. *Enjoy!*

reuben soup

The Reuben Sandwich has to be one of my all-time favorites. If you go to cavegirlcuisine.com, you'll find my Reuben Meatballs and Reuben Benedict. So, Reuben Soup? Why not! This is the only recipe in the book that has heavy cream added as an optional ingredient. If your gut health can handle a little dairy, this is the soup to splurge on!

ingredients

2 teaspoons bacon grease, or preferred cooking oil

1 medium onion, diced

2 celery stalks, diced

½ pound pastrami or corned beef, sliced or diced

4 cups beef broth

2 cups sauerkraut, drained

½ teaspoon ground mustard

1 teaspoon caraway seeds

½ cup organic heavy cream, optional

directions

In a soup pot or Dutch oven over medium-high heat, cook bacon grease, onion, and celery for a minute or two. Add pastrami. Continue to cook until onion is translucent.

Add broth, scraping any bits from bottom of pot. Add sauerkraut, ground mustard, and caraway seeds. Bring to a boil. Reduce heat and simmer covered for 20 minutes.

Whisk in optional heavy cream. Continue to simmer for 10 minutes. *Enjoy!*

Cavegirl Tip: *Instead of purchasing your pastrami pre-sliced, buy it at the meat counter and ask the deli clerk to cut the meat on blade 5 for a thicker cut.*

roasted cauliflower and bacon soup

This is absolutely a fan favorite. The base is flavorful and creamy and is topped off with the saltiness and fattiness of the bacon. Don't forget to read your bacon labels…some brands are laden with sugar.

ingredients

1 small head cauliflower, chopped

1 yellow onion, peeled and roughly chopped

4–6 cloves of garlic, peeled and halved

1–2 tablespoons avocado oil, or preferred oil

3 tablespoons ghee or real butter

3 celery stalks, chopped

1 tablespoon Italian Seasoning

1 teaspoon cassava flour or arrowroot flour

1 slice of bacon, finely diced

4 cups broth of choice

2–3 teaspoons sea salt, to taste

1 teaspoon ground pepper

6 slices of bacon, garnish

directions

Preheat oven to 350 degrees Fahrenheit.

Place cauliflower, onion, and garlic in a large baking dish. Drizzle with 1–2 tablespoons of oil. Bake for 30 minutes. Remove from oven and set aside.

In a soup pot or Dutch oven, place butter and celery, Italian seasoning, flour, and bacon on medium heat until butter is melted and celery is tender.

Add cauliflower mixture, broth, salt, and pepper. Bring to a boil. Reduce heat and let simmer for 30 minutes.

Using an immersion blender, blend ingredients until smooth. Taste broth and add additional salt if necessary. (An alternative is to transfer small batches to a stand blender, and blend until smooth).

In the meantime, cook the remaining 6 slices of bacon until crisp. Set aside.

Serve soup and crumble bacon on each bowl as a garnish with parsley and chopped scallions. *Enjoy!*

saffron and mussels soup

This bowl of soup is pure decadence. The cauliflower lends creaminess and silkiness to the base and the hint of saffron gives this dish a mildly earthy and indescribable quality. The common mussels bring it back home with their affordable price, but they have the elegance of a simple French classic.

ingredients

3 pounds mussels

4 slices bacon
(or two thick slices), diced

1 onion, diced

4 cups chicken or veggie broth

1 small head
cauliflower, chopped

Pinch of saffron threads
(about ¼ teaspoon)

2–3 cloves of garlic, minced

1 teaspoon sea salt

1 teaspoon ground white pepper

6-ounce can tomato paste

directions

Clean mussels. Submerge in a bowl of cold water for 20 minutes. Discard water, clean mussels of any additional debris, and remove beards and brown threads, if necessary. Some come already debearded, so you may be able to skip this step. Using fresh water, submerge mussels again for about 10–15 minutes.

In a soup pot or Dutch oven over medium heat, cook bacon to render some fat. Add onion and sauté until translucent. Stir in broth, cauliflower, saffron, garlic, salt, pepper, and tomato paste. Bring to a boil. Reduce heat and simmer covered for 25 minutes. Using an immersion blender, blend ingredients until smooth. (An alternative is to transfer small batches to a stand blender, and blend until smooth). Taste. Add additional salt if necessary.

Add mussels to soup and turn up heat to medium. Cover and continue to cook for 5 minutes. Discard any mussels that do not open.

Ladle soup into bowls. Serve with an additional bowl for emptied shells. *Enjoy!*

Cavegirl Side Story: *Years ago, my husband and I were stationed in Germany, and we took a side trip to the Bordeaux region of France. While there we tasted wine, ate great food with friends, and visited this little market in the middle of town. While my friends were buying what-nots and jewelry, I purchased this itty-bitty container of saffron, or safran, as it was written on my little container. This sat in the back on my spice drawer for years. I think I was afraid to use it because I might lose my memories. Well, I broke it out for this recipe. I have to say, the saffron was still as vibrant and beautiful as it should be. I will continue to use my saffron, but I think I'll always store these precious little threads in my special container.*

scallop chowder

If you don't have a problem with white potatoes, go ahead and use some in place of the rutabaga. However, they both have that similar starchy feel in your mouth. Depending on your dietary needs, rutabagas are lower in both calories and carbohydrates. You can also do a mix if you'd like to reap the benefits of the macronutrients in both. Parsnips and sweet potatoes could also give a fun twist to this chowder.

ingredients

4 strips uncured bacon, diced

1 pound bay scallops

8 ounces white mushrooms, quartered

3 celery stalks, chopped

1 medium onion, diced

3.5 cups rutabaga, peeled and diced

1 tablespoon fresh thyme leaves, plus extra for garnish

¼ teaspoon smoked paprika

8 ounces clam juice

¼ cup dry white wine, or additional broth

4 cups veggie or chicken broth

1 tablespoon cooking Sherry

Sea salt and ground pepper

directions

In a soup pot or Dutch oven, cook bacon until crisp. Set aside on a paper towel-lined plate.

Cook scallops in same pot with bacon grease for about 3 minutes, stirring once halfway through cooking time until scallops are cooked and opaque through the center. Remove scallops and set aside.

Add mushrooms, celery, and onion to same pot. Cook until onions are translucent.

Add remaining ingredients (except for scallops, bacon, and cooking Sherry).

Bring to boil. Let simmer for 30 minutes. Using an immersion blender, blend just enough to make broth a little creamy but still leaving soup chunky.

Add scallops and cooking Sherry. Continue to cook until scallops are heated through.

Spoon your scallop chowder into bowls. Garnish with bacon and additional thyme leaves. *Enjoy!*

shrimp egg drop soup

This is a very simple yet elegant dish. Make sure you mix the egg into the broth while the broth is heated; otherwise, it will just make a creamy soup. You want the heated broth so that you'll get those egg ribbons. Also, if this is a soup that you are freezing for later, skip the egg step and do this part when you are ready to reheat and eat it.

ingredients

1 cup green onions, sliced (white and green parts)

1 tablespoon fresh ginger (about a 1-inch knob), minced

2 tablespoons cassava flour or arrowroot flour

1 tablespoon coconut aminos

½ teaspoon sea salt

¼ teaspoon white pepper

2 cloves of garlic, minced

4 cups chicken broth

2 large eggs

¾ pound medium shrimp, cooked, peeled, and deveined

directions

In a soup pot or Dutch oven over high heat, add onions, ginger, flour, coconut aminos, salt, pepper, garlic, and chicken broth. Whisk ingredients to distribute the flour. Bring to boil and then reduce heat. Simmer covered for 15 minutes. Taste broth. Add additional salt if necessary.

Whisk eggs in a small bowl. Slowly drizzle eggs into soup. I like to pour my eggs over my whisk so it creates strands.

Add shrimp to the soup. Continue to cook for approximately 5 minutes until shrimp are opaque and cooked through. *Enjoy!*

simple broccoli and carrot soup

Are you in a rush? Need a quick go-to soup recipe? This is your recipe! Quick! Get to cookin'...this one is almost done!

ingredients

3 tablespoons ghee
or real butter

1 head broccoli, chopped

3 carrots, peeled and diced

1 small onion, diced

3 garlic cloves, minced

1 tablespoon capers

Pinch of red pepper flakes

1 teaspoon sea salt

3 cups veggie or chicken broth
+ 1 cup, if needed

Ground pepper to taste

directions

In a soup pot or Dutch oven, melt ghee over medium heat. Add broccoli, carrots, onion, garlic, capers, red pepper flakes, and one teaspoon of salt. Sauté until onions are translucent.

Add 3 cups broth to pot. Bring to a boil. Reduce heat and let simmer covered for 30 minutes. Using an immersion blender (or a stand blender in batches), blend ingredients until smooth.

Because of the different sized heads of broccoli and carrots, only add 3 cups of broth at first. If soup is too thick, continue to add remaining broth to desired consistency. Add additional salt if necessary. Garnish each bowl of soup with freshly ground pepper. *Enjoy!*

spicy avocado florentine soup

This rich and silky soup is loaded with flavor but even more with nutrition. The avocados and spinach are powerhouse foods loaded with phytonutrients, making this a healthy meal choice.

ingredients

3 tablespoons ghee or real butter

2 avocados, peeled, pitted, and diced

1 jalapeño, stem removed and roughly chopped

½ medium onion, diced

1 celery stalk, diced

1 tablespoon thyme leaves, plus more for garnish

4 cups veggie broth

2 handfuls baby spinach (about 5 ounces)

Sea salt and ground pepper, to taste

directions

In a soup pot or Dutch oven, melt ghee over medium heat. Add avocados, jalapeño, onion, celery, and thyme leaves. Sauté until onions are translucent.

Stir in veggie broth. Bring to a boil. Reduce heat and simmer covered for 25 minutes. Add spinach and continue to simmer until spinach wilts. Using an immersion blender (or a stand mixer in batches), blend soup until smooth. Season with salt and pepper, to taste.

Serve with thyme leaves on top for garnish and maybe even a little chopped crisp bacon! *Enjoy!*

spicy thai lobster soup (lobster tom kha)

The first time I tried Tom Kha was at a little local restaurant in St. Louis. It was love at first taste, and I've been cooking foods in spicy coconut milk broth ever since. Some of my ingredients probably aren't truly authentic to the region, but I think my Paleo version will get you where you need to be when craving this Thai delight!

ingredients

3 tablespoons ghee or real butter

5–6 scallions, whites and greens divided, sliced

5 ounces shiitake mushrooms, sliced

4 cups veggie broth, or broth of choice

4 small uncooked lobster tails (about 1.5 cups of cooked meat)

2–3 garlic cloves, minced

1 teaspoon coconut aminos

1 teaspoon lime zest

1 tablespoon red curry paste

2 tablespoons minced lemongrass (the soft inner layer)

2 teaspoons Sriracha, or preferred hot sauce

¼ teaspoon ginger, finely chopped

1 tablespoon cooking Sherry

1 cup coconut milk

1 handful cilantro leaves, plus extra for garnish

directions

In a soup pot or Dutch oven over medium heat, melt ghee. Saute' the whites of the scallions and mushrooms until scallions are tender.

Add broth. Add lobster tails. Bring to a boil. Reduce to a simmer and cook until tail shells just turn red.

Cut lobster tails down the center and scoop out slightly undercooked lobster meat. Set meat aside. Place the large lobster shell portions back into the broth. Bring to boil. Reduce to a simmer and cook covered for 30 minutes.

Remove lobster shells from broth and discard. Whisk in coconut aminos, lime zest, red curry paste, lemongrass, Sriracha, and ginger. Heat on medium-low for 10 minutes.

Add Sherry, coconut milk, chopped green part of scallions, and a handful of cilantro. Whisk together and continue to cook for 5 minutes. Add lobster meat. Continue to cook for an additional 5 minutes.

Serve immediately. Garnish with additional cilantro. *Enjoy!*

Cavegirl Tip: *Because half of the population has a DNA predisposition whereby cilantro tastes soapy, substitute basil or Thai basil in this recipe for a tasty alternative if you are in that 50 percent!*

strawberry-tomato basil soup with balsamic drizzle

This soup was inspired by a simple dish in the summer that many enjoy. Fresh strawberries tossed with balsamic vinegar alongside a glass of crisp white wine is such a fresh indulgence. Because I am not a fan of sweet soups, the tomatoes help round out the flavors of this elegant meal.

ingredients

1 tablespoon avocado oil, or preferred cooking oil

2 carrots, peeled and diced

1 small shallot, diced

1 red bell pepper, or color of choice, seeded and diced

1 cup strawberries, stems removed

28-ounce can organic diced tomatoes, including juice

15 basil leaves, plus more for garnish

3 cups veggie or chicken broth

Sea salt and ground pepper, to taste

Balsamic vinegar, to drizzle

directions

In a soup pot or Dutch oven, heat oil over medium heat and sauté carrots, shallot, and red pepper until shallots are translucent.

Add strawberries, tomatoes, basil leaves, broth, and a pinch or two of salt and pepper. Bring to a boil. Reduce heat and simmer covered for 30 minutes.

Using an immersion blender, blend ingredients until smooth. An alternative is to transfer small batches to a stand blender and blend until smooth.

Taste soup and season with additional salt, if necessary.

Ladle soup into bowls. Garnish with a light drizzle of balsamic vinegar and fresh basil. *Enjoy!*

summer squash soup

If you are into gardening (or if your generous neighbor is), you are familiar with that time of year when you are overwhelmed with crookneck squash. Although steamed squash and squash patties are sometimes staples during this time of year, I wanted to try something new with my harvest. This is one of my personal favorites, and the bacon and chili pepper really bring the flavor profile to a new level. The Anaheim chili pepper is very mild, so you can always substitute hotter pepper varieties.

ingredients

2 pieces bacon, diced

½ large red onion, diced

2 celery stalks, chopped

1–2 Anaheim chili peppers, seeded and diced

½ teaspoon sea salt

½ teaspoon garlic salt

2 teaspoons red pepper flakes

1 tablespoon parsley flakes

4 cups veggie or chicken broth

4 cups summer squash or zucchini (about 2-3), roughly chopped

1 parsnip, peeled and diced, or a small turnip

Sea salt and ground pepper, to taste

Optional garnishes:
Cooked, crumbled bacon and fresh parsley

directions

In a soup pot or Dutch oven, place bacon, onion, celery, Anaheim chili pepper, sea salt, garlic salt, red pepper flakes, and parsley flakes. Cook on medium heat until onion is tender.

Add broth, squash and parsnip. Bring to a boil. Reduce to low and simmer for one hour. Using an immersion blender (or transferring batches to a stand-up blender), puree soup ingredients. Add salt and pepper to taste. *Enjoy!*

thai fish and sweet potato noodle soup

Never discuss religion, politics, or…cilantro. Apparently, the latter really stirs up some heated discussions! Many Thai soups contain cilantro; however, it is one of those herbs that you either love or hate, so I used baby kale instead for my haters. According to many studies, the dislike of cilantro may be in your DNA, and you are predisposed for it to taste "soapy."

ingredients

13.5-ounce can coconut milk

2 cups veggie broth

1-inch knob of ginger, sliced in thin circles

1 tablespoon coconut aminos

1 tablespoon fish sauce

1 teaspoon raw honey

3 cloves of garlic, halved

1 tablespoon peppercorns

½ lime, peeled and quartered

1 cup shiitakes, or mushrooms of choice, diced

¼ cup scallions (the green portion), sliced plus extra for garnish

1 large sweet potato, spiraled or julienned

4 3-ounce cod fillets

2 tablespoons sesame oil

directions

In a large saucepan over high heat, add coconut milk, veggie broth, ginger, coconut aminos, fish sauce, honey, garlic, peppercorns, and lime. Bring to a boil. Reduce heat and simmer covered for 20 minutes. Strain solids out of broth and discard. Transfer broth back into saucepan.

Add mushrooms and scallions to soup base. Simmer for 5 minutes. Add spiraled sweet potato. Cover and continue cooking until sweet potato is tender (about another 5 minutes).

During the last minutes of cooking the soup, heat sesame oil in a small skillet. Cook cod fillets for approximately 4 minutes per side, depending on thickness. You want it to be opaque throughout without overcooking. Remove from heat and transfer fish to a plate so it won't continue to cook.

Ladle soup and noodles into four bowls. Place a cod fillet in the middle of each bowl. Garnish with additional sliced scallions. *Enjoy!*

white chicken chili

Busy?? This is your recipe. Take 10 minutes in the morning to throw everything in the slow cooker. Come home to an incredible-smelling home and a warm, comforting meal. The recipe calls for a 6-hour cooking time, but if it goes for 8 hours, don't worry about it. Your chicken probably won't have to be fork-separated, as it will already have fallen apart, but the flavor will be there.

ingredients

1.5 pounds chicken breasts, thighs, or a combination

1 medium onion, diced

1 yellow bell pepper, seeded and diced

1 jalapeño, seeded and diced

1 handful parsley leaves (about ¾ cup)

4-ounce can fire-roasted diced green chili peppers

1 tablespoon cassava flour or coconut flour

1 teaspoon sea salt

1 teaspoon white pepper

1 teaspoon ground cumin

1 teaspoon chili powder

1 teaspoon dried mint leaves

4 cups chicken broth

directions

Layer chicken on bottom of a 6-quart slow cooker.

Add onion, bell pepper, jalapeño, parsley, green chili peppers, flour, and seasonings. Sprinkle flour over layers. Add chicken broth.

Cook for 6 hours on low heat. Using two forks, pull apart chicken in slow cooker. Taste broth. Add additional salt, if necessary. *Enjoy!*

wild mushroom soup

This soup is flexible, as my grocer always has different wild mushrooms available. If you only have button and baby bella mushrooms at your fingertips, go for it...this recipe will work just fine. But, if you have a chance to branch out, the flavors of the less available varieties can lend such an earthiness and different flavor to your meal.

ingredients

3 tablespoons ghee or real butter

1 leek, sliced

2 cups mixed mushrooms, your choice (I used bella, oyster, and shiitake)

½ rutabaga, peeled and diced

2 celery stalks, diced

2 cloves of garlic, halved

1 tablespoon thyme leaves

1 teaspoon sea salt

1 teaspoon ground pepper

4 cups mushroom or chicken broth

1 teaspoon cooking Sherry

directions

In a soup pot or Dutch oven, melt ghee over medium heat. Add leek, 1 cup of mushrooms, rutabaga, celery, garlic, thyme, salt, and pepper. Sauté until leeks are tender.

Add broth. Bring to a boil. Reduce heat and simmer covered for 15 minutes. Using an immersion blender (or a stand blender in batches), blend until smooth.

Add remaining mushrooms and Sherry. Season with additional salt and pepper, to taste. Continue to simmer covered for an additional 15 minutes. *Enjoy!*

zucchini and tomato soup

The garden-fresh flavor of this soup helps embrace the end of summer with the abundance of zucchini. Even though this is a low-calorie soup, the heartiness of the vegetables fills both the body and soul!

ingredients

1 tablespoon avocado oil, or preferred cooking oil

1 medium onion, diced

2 celery stalks, diced

3 medium zucchini, diced

13.5-ounce can diced tomatoes

4 tablespoons tomato paste

1 teaspoon Sriracha, or preferred hot sauce

¼ teaspoon celery seed

½ teaspoon dried oregano

½ teaspoon dried basil

1 teaspoon sea salt

3 cups veggie or chicken broth

directions

In a soup pot or Dutch oven, heat oil over medium heat. Sauté onions and celery until onions are translucent.

Add remaining ingredients. Bring to a boil. Reduce heat and simmer covered for 30 minutes. Taste broth and add additional salt if necessary. *Enjoy!*

index

www.ingramcontent.com/pod-product-compliance
Lightning Source LLC
LaVergne TN
LVHW070142110826
845147LV00002B/308

9780990382379